T033490O

GROUP EFFORTS: CHANGING PUBLIC SPACE

Hayal Pozanti and Todd Shalom

Greta Hansen, Kyung Jae Kim, and Adam Koogler

Karen Finley

Mabel O. Wilson

EDITED BY GAVIN BROWNING

GSAPP BOOKS, 2015

The GSAPP Transcripts series is a curated record of the major events that take place at the Columbia University Graduate School of Architecture, Planning and Preservation. Embracing the simple idea that publication is the act of making something public, these books form a channel through which the discourse internal to the school enters the public arena of architectural media and ideas, in the form of edited talks and symposia. In each case, the original lectures and discussions at the core of these books are augmented with supplementary material, additional imagery, and critical commentary, expanding their debates and provocations beyond the confines of the lecture hall.

Rem Koolhaas
Preservation Is Overtaking Us
with a supplement by
Jorge Otero-Pailos (2014)

Yvonne Farrell
and Shelley McNamara
Dialogue and Translation:
Grafton Architects
with an essay by
Kenneth Frampton (2014)

2000+: The Urgencies of
Architectural Theory
ed. James Graham (2015)

Group Efforts: Changing
Public Space
ed. Gavin Browning, with an
essay by Mabel Wilson (2015)

Angelo Bucci
The Dissolution of Buildings
with an essay by
Kenneth Frampton (2015)

4
INTRODUCTION
Gavin Browning

9
SUBJECTIVE CONTOURS
Hayal Pozanti and Todd Shalom

25
INFLATABLE GENERAL
ASSEMBLY
Greta Hansen, Kyung Jae Kim,
and Adam Koogler

41
MANDALA: REIMAGINING
COLUMBUS CIRCLE
Karen Finley

71
MINGLING IN CURIOUS
AND UNCANNY MANNERS
Mabel O. Wilson

INTRO-DUCTION
Gavin Browning

Public space is constantly changing in New York City. Busy intersections become pedestrian plazas, desolate strips of waterfront grow into verdant parks, and traffic is redirected to make way for festivals and parades. Buildings are dismantled and built back up—sometimes enhancing surroundings with them—and rents continue to rise.

Group Efforts: Changing Public Space traces perceptual, not physical, changes to public space. The three projects described within this volume did not break ground or leave marks on our city, yet the transformations they effected are real. They required only the willingness of individuals to gather and do things together.

I commissioned these works over the course of a year at the Graduate School of Architecture, Planning and Preservation (GSAPP) of Columbia University. They appeared within the framework of a series of lectures, debates, and symposia on the built environment, but unlike those traditional formats, they happened in smaller groups away from the campus. Two of the three were collaborations with Elastic City, an organization dedicated to making "its audience active participants in an ongoing poetic exchange with the places we live in and visit" through walks led by artists.

The people interviewed here work across media, and they translated their aesthetic sensibilities into group experience. Hayal Pozanti is a painter and Todd Shalom creates participatory performances; Greta Hansen, Kyung Jae Kim, and Adam Koogler are architects and designers; Karen Finley is a visual and performance artist. At the time, I did not see their work as a trilogy, even though that is how they are presented here. Rather, I viewed them as unique experiences—three distinct windows through which to see the myriad forces shaping public space and its use today.

Others have done this before them. In the 1970s, William H. Whyte and a team of researchers used time-lapse filmmaking techniques to explore how people used the plaza of the Seagram Building, observing that they made the modernist space their own. In *The Social Life of Small Urban Spaces*, Whyte notes how the harmonious arrangement of objects can facilitate civic exchange and daily dramas. New Yorkers sunbathed on ledges, catcalled from stairs and standpipes, fashioned ad hoc desks from trash can lids, and tied their shoelaces on fire hydrants. But "[w]hat attracts people most, it would appear, is other people."[1]

Many of the resulting urban design recommendations were adopted by New York City, leading to the creation of lively, accessible, and populated public spaces that offer relief from the grid and the grind. Today Whyte's conclusions might seem obvious. On a hot summer day, who wouldn't value a shady place to sit and relax, to drink from a water fountain, admire beautiful landscaping and trees, and perhaps meet someone new?

But in the decades since this canonical study, much has changed about the funding and oversight of the public places in which we gather. Many of them now privatized, the quality of amenities and number of people using them are no longer reliable metrics of their publicness. In *Rebel Cities*, geographer David Harvey notes that in the mid-1980s, "neoliberal urban policy concluded that redistributing wealth to less advantaged neighborhoods, cities, and regions was futile, and that resources should instead be channeled to dynamic 'entrepreneurial' growth poles."[2] Just like the buildings that house multinational corporations, the privately owned public plazas, atria, and arcades that surround them are embedded within the movement of global capital—flows that exclude as they expand. From the shadows of the Time Warner Center at 10 Columbus Circle, Karen Finley suggests ways "to include more voices" in our experience of public space. "I'm applying psychological, therapeutic, and religious practice → p. 44 to the city as a way of diagnosing. The mandala will reveal, and the person reading through it will speak."

Parks and streets are also stewarded by the private sector. Manhattan's celebrated Bryant Park and High Line are operated by wealthy non-profit conservancies, while Business Improvement Districts (BIDs) balkanize the city into branded swathes. The care for local public goods such as clean sidewalks and well-lit streets has been outsourced. According to the New

York City Department of Small Business Services, Union Square Partnership, Fulton Mall Improvement Association, Bayside Village, and sixty-seven other such public-private partnerships across the five boroughs invest more than $100 million annually in district-specific programs and services. Inevitably, disparity arises. The essay at the back of this book by Mabel O. Wilson explores these uneven distributions for political agency and democratic urban life. She contrasts their implications with those of Inflatable General Assembly (IGA), a pneumatic pavilion for spontaneous political activity by Greta Hansen, Kyung Jae Kim, and Adam Koogler. With the IGA, "[Y]ou make your own space," says Hansen. "If you're → p. 38 here, you're blowing it up. You're part of the constant creation of the space itself."

I see the outsourcing of care as emblematic of other trends in our individualistic society: skepticism of state-provided aid; fear of those who are different; the drive to amass personal instead of collective wealth. The projects described here do not claim to redress the inequities that foreclose opportunities for so many. But crucially, I think, they ask us to be vulnerable and to help each other.

"Please take care of your partner." Hayal → p. 17 Pozanti and Todd Shalom challenge us to close our eyes and traverse a city block, guided only by the sounds around us and someone by our side. "Walk toward what you want to listen to. Your ears are microphones. Feel free to take the arm or hand of your partner."

Then, we switch roles. The blind leads the sighted toward a destination we will determine together in time. Eyes closed, we see the world anew.

1   William H. Whyte, The Social Life of Small Urban Spaces (New York: Project for Public Spaces, 2001), 19.

2   David Harvey, Rebel Cities: From the Right to the City to the Urban Revolution (New York: Verso, 2012), 29.

"Our eyes
are growing bigger
by the minute
while our
fingertips shrink."

SUBJECTIVE CONTOURS
Hayal Pozanti and Todd Shalom

Hayal Pozanti and Todd Shalom discuss Subjective Contours.

HAYAL POZANTI: I started thinking about "flattening space" by looking at art online. Some installations or artworks are made to be looked at in a flat way, on a screen. It's thinking about space in terms of props; placing objects according to how they would be photographed rather than experienced in real life. They might be arranged to create a beautiful painting when shot from a specific angle.

On Saturday, October 13, 2013, Hayal Pozanti and Todd Shalom led two groups of twelve on Subjective Contours, a participatory walk through Manhattan's West Village, at 2pm and 5pm. The meeting point was the northwest corner of Waverly Place and 6th Avenue. The walk lasted eighty-five minutes and required the following materials: acetate film, a camera, colored tape, envelopes, markers, scissors, stamps, and string. The text that runs alongside this interview was written by the artists. Unless noted, the following photographs were taken along this walk.

Objects are fleeting, and we live in an ephemeral world of screens. We don't always get to experience buildings. They may be torn down, bombed down, so when we look at them we look at images. Flattening gives access to those who cannot physically grasp them in three dimensions.

The buildings that appeal to us may have sculptural qualities that work when viewed online. I think whichever three-dimensional space translates best onto a two-dimensional screen is what will circulate the most.

GAVIN BROWNING: You flatten space on canvas. What happens when you flatten urban space?

POZANTI: It follows the same logic. You can flatten a building or a block by photographing it at various angles, but only one angle will successfully convey its dimensionality. The angle really matters.

BROWNING: How so?

POZANTI: Flattening is subjective. A subjective contour! I made a sculpture titled "Object 001" that is meant to be viewed and photographed from one specific angle. I drew the object in SketchUp. Then I built and painted it according to the correct shadows and photographed it from that angle. It's a vessel that carries all of the information you need about the object in a flat way, and I thought more about how it would look on a screen than in real life.

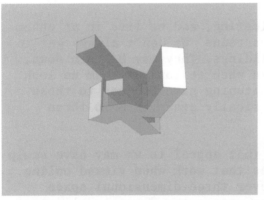

Left: SketchUp drawing for "Object 001." Right: "Object 001."

TODD SHALOM: A big part of flattening is removing depth. But a big part of the participatory walk form is to take a traditionally fact-based tour and give it another kind of depth, in a hands-on way. That brings people together and helps them experience both each other and a place from new perspectives.

POZANTI: For example, this composition doesn't have to be about a building receding. If we take away the background and street, it could be a mountain, or a triangle with vertical lines. Suddenly, three-dimensional spaces that are part of our world have a figure-ground relationship.

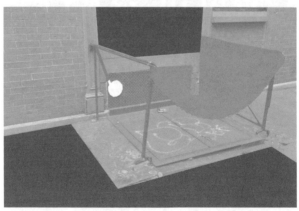

Drawings for Subjective Contours by Hayal Pozanti.

SHALOM: Outside, I'm surrounded by things. I know they exist in three-dimensional space because I can touch them. But I want to experience a place differently. When flattening space as a group, there's a collective choice to suspend disbelief.

Do you remember Magic Eye, the prints that were sold in malls? If you looked at them in a certain way, an image would jump out.

BROWNING: Yes, but I could never see them.

SHALOM: I could never see them either, and I've always wanted to. We want to experience phenomena. Maybe we're using a prop to access it, maybe not. Flattening space introduces the idea that, without drugs, you can experience an altered state with your senses alone.

Magic Eye.

POZANTI: In a group, people inform each other. They held up their drawings, "Look at it this way, look at it that way," and others saw things from new angles.

Analog Photoshopping → fig. 001
Waverly Place and Gay Street
Markers, Transparencies, Camera

Ten minutes

There are multiple depths of space, and many angles through which to view. Let's look at the compelling shape of the Northern Dispensary.

1. Circle the building and find the best angle for you.
2. Create a frame on the transparency using a marker.
3. Sketch the contours, such as the outlines of buildings. Forget depth; envision the world flat like on a screen.
4. Fill the contours with color or patterns.

SHALOM: We stood behind them to get their angle. We tried to mimic their height or stance in order to get their vantage point, their perception, to see each other's perspective. But you can only get it by being them. Everyone will have a different experience, and we learned how each perspective is unique.

POZANTI: People are singular walking angles. They flatten space individually.

SHALOM: No matter how hard you try to see through someone else's eyes, you're going to see things your own way.

BROWNING: Of all the neighborhoods in New York, why flatten the West Village?

POZANTI: The West Village is an interesting part of New York because there's no grid. Buildings overlap, streets crisscross, and the texture is more chaotic. With the grid, you're mostly frontal. You see façades, right angles. What you see is what you get. Coming from Istanbul, I'm familiar with the feeling of being lost. Cab drivers wouldn't know where to go if you gave them an address. It's like there are no addresses; you always describe a location. That McDonald's in Beşiktaş. The West Village feels more Eurasian.

SHALOM: For me, it's a charged place. I came out around there, kissed guys in the crevices of its buildings, and led Elastic City walks that have listened to sounds in its gay bars, video stores, and alleyways. The West Village is beautifully overloaded, and Hayal encouraged me to think about it in a visual way.

Our planning process was to get lost in the neighborhood and see where it would take us. We ended at Julius'. Normally, I would focus on the

Scoring 7th Avenue
7th Avenue between Waverly Place and Greenwich Avenue

Five minutes

Look at this strip of buildings. If you look horizontally from left to right, the windows are sometimes aligned, and then they fall out of alignment. To us, these windows can be read like a musical score. We have divided the floors of the buildings in front of us into three sections: top, middle, and bottom. Each group will take a section.

1. In your group, count the number of windows running across your section.
2. Create a sound for the windows in your section.
3. Moving left to right across the block, sing each window as a beat.
4. Wherever there is no window, be quiet.

As a group, let's sing from left to right at the same time. We will provide a rhythm with our hands like a metronome to help keep everyone on track.

5. Repeat twice.

historical meaning
of a place like that—
how it is the longest
still-operating
gay bar in New York,
how it hosted a
Sip-In in 1966 that
helped galvanize
the gay community
before Stonewall.

POZANTI: But I was
drawn to the exterior.
The wall is like an
AbEx painting. It has
beautiful hand marks,
and following them
is like watching some-
body build in real
time. Fascinating.
Tactility is import-
ant because we spend
so much time in front
of screens. We're
touching fewer things
and losing touch with
other senses. Our eyes
are growing bigger by
the minute while our
fingertips shrink.

BROWNING: The neigh-
borhood is a case
study for historic
preservationists. Its
fabric and character
are protected, but

Listen → fig. 002
West 13th Street between 7th and
8th Avenues

Ten minutes

1. Find a partner and decide who
   wants to have their eyes closed and
   who wants to have their eyes open.
2. Person with your eyes closed: walk
   toward what you want to listen to.
   Your ears are microphones. Feel
   free to take the arm or hand of
   your partner.
3. Person with your eyes open: please
   take care of your partner. Make
   sure they do not walk into traffic
   or bump into anything.
4. Do not talk to each other unless
   it's urgent.
5. We will walk straight down this
   street to its end, then reverse roles.

for whom? Does Subjective Contours take it back?

SHALOM: The West Village is beyond gentrified. It's comfortable to the point of being exclusionary, except on the margins. You can express yourself at the piers, and the police allow rowdiness in the park by Stonewall. But otherwise, there aren't a lot of places where people can freely hang out. The West Village is gorgeous, inaccessible, privileged, and more European. It's the ideal Manhattan neighborhood for someone who can afford to live in a beautiful bubble, and it's asking for an intervention.

POZANTI: While we were planning our walk in New York, activists in Istanbul occupied Taksim Gezi Park. They protested the demolition of an old bakery,

Touch → fig. 003
Julius', 159 West 10th Street

Five minutes

Imagine yourself making this wall.

1. Mimic the actions of the builders who stuccoed this wall.
2. Place your hands on the wall. How did they move their hands and bodies?
3. Find various shapes inside this façade.

Occupy Space → fig. 004
Bank Street and Greenwich Avenue
Colored tape

Five minutes

Imagine yourself making this wall.

1. Enter the cavity of this building.
2. Using just your bodies, fill as much space as possible.
3. Create a web with your arms and legs.

We will help you cast it in tape.

the Emek cinema,
and a historic park
for more malls that
nobody really wanted
but would profit a
few. People reclaimed
their streets. Walking
as a group reclaims
streets, too. We have
as much access to
this street as anyone
else; we will dis-
rupt, interrupt, and
use it to our will. On
the day of our walk,
part of 7th Avenue was
closed for construc-
tion, and a makeshift
sidewalk had been
demarcated by jer-
sey barriers. We moved
through it in a zig-
zag. We didn't have
to walk in a straight
line. We could walk in
a zigzag because the
street is ours, too.

SHALOM: It was simul-
taneously playful and
aggressive.

POZANTI: It invited
oncoming pedestrians
to zigzag along
with us, and it felt
like a game. Even

Wish Generator → fig. 005
West 12th Street and 7th Avenue
Pen, Envelope, Stamp

Seven minutes

Take a moment and think about what
you wish for the neighborhood.

1. Whisper your wish into the utility
   box affixed to the side of this building. The building will process your
   wish and deposit it in the ashtray
   affixed to the other side.
2. Pick up your wish from the ashtray
   and hold on to it.

Let's walk down the street to the
mailbox.

3. One at a time, place your wish into
   this envelope.

Who should we send our wishes to?

4. Stamp, address, and mail the
   envelope.

19

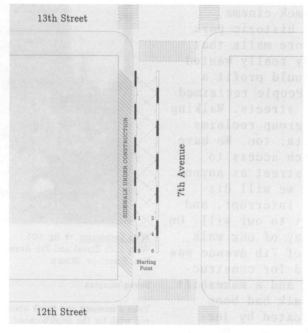

Zigzag
7th Avenue between West 12th and
West 13th Streets

Two minutes

Stand in two parallel lines on different
sides of a sidewalk.

1. Walk forward to your right until
   you hit the barrier while the person
   opposite you walks forward to
   the left.
2. When you hit the barrier, walk
   forward to your left until you hit
   the barrier while the person opposite
   you walks forward to the right.

Zigzag up the block.

the construction mate-
rials were playful.
Their orange-white,
orange-white pattern
gave us something to
bounce off.

BROWNING: Historic
preservation freezes
urban shapes in time,
but the group recon-
figured them.

POZANTI: I think
about generating new
shapes twenty-four
hours a day, and it's
how I want people
to see the world. I
wanted to try making
them in an urban land-
scape. Our subjective
contours are outlines
of new shapes. They
aren't ones you could
identify from basic
geometry, a triangle
here, a hexagon there.
They combine these
shapes to invent ones
that haven't existed before.

String Along → fig. 006
Jane Street between Greenwich and
8th Avenues
Colored Tape, Scissors, String

Ten minutes

Let's string these tree guards together
and flatten the space in between them.

1. Wrap the string around the
   tree guards and cut the string
   as necessary.
2. Arrange the string sculpture
   as desired.

BROWNING: Did we paint a painting?

POZANTI: By flattening space together, we
created sketches for paintings that are yet
to exist. Our role as artists is to provide

another outlook,
another view. It
doesn't have to be
an object. It can
be an experience.

SHALOM: When people
walk by buildings,
they can sing them.

I Do Declare
West 12th and West 4th Streets
Markers, Transparencies

Eight minutes

1. Walk around this intersection and
   look at all the text around you.
2. Glean text that you like, and form
   that text into a poetic declaration.
3. Write your phrase in any manner
   on the transparency.

When everyone is done, we will
share our transparencies, holding
it from your desired angle, and we'll
get behind you and read it.

"Our role could
be to create
instructions."

INFLATABLE GENERAL ASSEMBLY
Greta Hansen, Kyung Jae Kim, and Adam Koogler

Common Practice (Greta Hansen, Kyung Jae Kim, and Adam Koogler) install Inflatable General Assembly.

KYUNG JAE KIM: In the beginning of the occupation of Zuccotti Park, things were calm. Michael Bloomberg cooperated with protestors. His plan seemed to be to allow them to stay until nature eventually swept them away. When winter comes, the people will go. We and other architects and planners were thinking of how to help them deal with dropping temperatures.

Common Practice's Inflatable General Assembly was inflated at Studio-X New York on Thursday, October 17, 2013, for the conversation Protest and Public Space with Hayrettin Günç, Selva Gürdoğan, Yates McKee, and Anya Schiffrin. It was re-inflated on Saturday, October 4, 2014 in Sara D. Roosevelt Park and Seward Park on Manhattan's Lower East Side. Unless noted, all photographs were taken on Saturday, October 4, 2014 in Sara D. Roosevelt Park and Seward Park.

ADAM KOOGLER: Winter was setting in, and there was a lot of rain. Protestors' tents would freeze to the pavement, and when they thawed, their stuff would get wet. We thought that if they could find a pallet in an alley in the Financial District, and if they could stuff it with plastic bags and cover it with cardboard, then they could create an insulated foundation that would keep them off the wet ground and enable them to endure harsher conditions than in a tent alone. It wouldn't cost anything out of pocket, and it wouldn't violate code.

"Protesters slept wrapped in blankets and sleeping bags, partly insulated from the chilly ground by pieces of cardboard scavenged from nearby stores.

"On Monday morning dozens of those scraps of cardboard doubled as signs, duct-taped to part of the park facing Liberty Street and emblazoned with handwritten messages including 'Kill the Zombie Banks,' 'I came here because I am scared for my country,' and 'End corporate welfare.'"
—Colin Moynihan, "Wall Street Protests Continue, With at Least 6 Arrested," New York Times, September 19, 2011

KIM: In New York City, a structure requires a permit if it is 120 square feet or larger. It'd

be illegal to build in a park. But because Zuccotti Park is a Privately Owned Public Space,
we didn't know the rules. If its foundation was
mobile, such as a pallet, we thought it would
be exempt.

KOOGLER: There are gaps within building code,
zoning, and property rights laws that allowed
for lightweight, non-structural solutions
for shelter and basic human needs within the
mini-society of Occupy Wall Street. The city
wasn't thinking that way. We saw opportunities
to use our professional knowledge to improve
the conditions on site, not by dictating in
a top-down way, but by transferring knowledge.
Our role could be to create instructions.

GRETA HANSEN: We dumbed down what an architect does. A construction document is a simple
set of instructions. They can do a lot, and
you don't need to spend any money on them.
They became our project in Zuccotti Park [123
Occupy] rather than building the pallets themselves, and our goal shifted from intervening
upon the physicality of the camp to communicat-
ing ideas within it.

HANSEN: The police cracked down on tents. They
said that a tarp with a pole was a structure.
So protesters tied tarps to trees, and then
the police said that the trees had to be protected. Anything with a pole or tied to a tree
was illegal. Because we love Archigram and Ant
Farm, inflatables were on our minds, and in our
research, we found that New York City Building
Code does not say a lot about them. They're
like building with bamboo. Not a lot is written

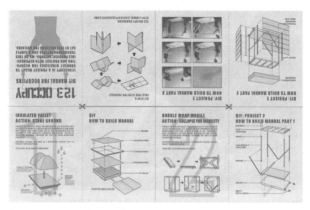

Common Practice's 123 Occupy pamphlet, 2011.

and their legality is hazy. So, what if we inflated a tent? The city couldn't say it was a structure because it wouldn't have any poles, even if it covered the entirety of the General Assembly in Zuccotti Park. We designed an inflatable to cover the width of the block between Liberty and Cedar Streets, with air being continuously refilled through thirty-six foot pumps.

KIM: It would require constant participation.

KOOGLER: Occupation is taxing. It wears on people and they need to constantly psych themselves up. Inflatables also require sustained effort, and I find interesting parallels between the two.

"The Constitution doesn't protect tents … it protects speech and assembly."
—Michael Bloomberg, October 17, 2011

"In this complex unity, we say yes to life. We say yes to happiness. We say yes to community. We say yes to education; to free education. Yes to economic and racial and gender and sexual equality. We say yes to the imagination. Yes to creativity. We say yes to hope, and yes to the future."
—Angela Davis, addressing Occupy Wall Street protestors, October 30, 2011

Small Inflatable General Assembly at the 13th International
Architecture Exhibition of the Venice Biennale, 2012.

HANSEN: The pallets provided shelter and kept
people in place. But the inflatable is a
different form of protest. It's a quick, effi-
cient, communicative way to take over space,
like putting up a sign.

KIM: We intended to make a symbolic gesture,
not occupy territory. The Inflatable General
Assembly would be a flag from the encampment
to the city outside, in the same way that pro-
democracy protestors used umbrellas in Hong
Kong in 2014. They created a beautiful canopy
to signal their presence.

GAVIN BROWNING: Did you make instructions for
this tent?

HANSEN: We did, and we followed them by cutting
pieces of plastic and sewing them together. But
they didn't work. We had been thinking in terms
of the tension and compression in a beam or a
column, and never having built a bubble before,
we imagined we could create a compression

column by simply filling a bag with air. But we found that structure comes from tension in the membrane material.

KOOGLER: Inflatables require an almost imperceptible difference in air pressure between their interior and exterior and the tiniest of membrane to separate the two.

HANSEN: We had been trying to create something dense. A bag filled with compressed air will accept weight; you can stack something on top of it. But the prototype we built with differential air pressure collapsed.

We realized we needed to work with the movement of air, following the instructions in the 1970s engineering book Principles of Pneumatic Architecture.

"Pneumatic construction possess[es] an individuality that is far removed from conventional structural techniques." —Roger N. Dent

Eclectic Electric Collective's Inflatable Cobblestone, Barcelona, 2012.

KOOGLER: We dug into the science and military-industrial history, then spent weeks laying out forms with jigs and ironing plastic together with parchment. It was a pattern-making exercise, like making a dress. But we were being such architects about it, exerting a lot of control. Even our methods of detailing and attachment were heavy-handed. In the end, we found that a roll of tape was the best thing.

"A 40-by-40 foot plastic bag was the theater, stage and prop yesterday for a chillingly realistic bit of theater about a day when the air becomes too polluted to breathe.

"'Air Emergency' was conceived and built by a Sausalito 'family' of dropout architects called Ant Farm. The commune, touring American campuses with their Clean Air Pod (CAP 1500) performed outdoors at the University of California campus as part of a three-day Environmental Teach-In.

"As an air raid siren drew U.C. students to lower Sproul Plaza, a monotone loudspeaker voice informed them that an 'air failure' had occurred and those who couldn't escape the pollution would die within fifteen minutes.

"The voice invited onlookers to take shelter in the CAP 1500 which, it said, had been tested 'in Akron under government contract.' The air system inflating CAP 1500 also screens out deadly pollutants, the voice said."
—"Breathing – That's Their Bag," Oakland Tribune, April 22, 1972 (Ant Farm and the Oakland Tribune intentionally dated this article two years in advance).

BROWNING: Inflatables have often been countercultural and event-based. Ant Farm built one at the Altamont Speedway Free Festival in 1969, and another at Sproul Plaza at University of California, Berkeley in 1970 to draw attention to environmental degradation.

HANSEN: There have been many playful and performative uses of inflatables. Eclectic Electric Collective inflated mirrored heat blankets into huge cobblestones that are thrown at protests. Like them, we're making something from marginal materials. Junk. Anyone can create one with little or no investment.

Ant Farm's Clean Air Pod (CAP 1500), Sproul Plaza, UC Berkeley, 1970.

HANSEN: Even permanent inflatable structures are event-based, such as stadiums for major sporting spectacles.

KOOGLER: Expo '70 in Osaka.

KIM: The circus.

KOOGLER: Architects often inflate temporary structures when renovating a building. The renovation may last for six months or one year, but it is framed as an event rather than a permanent condition.

HANSEN: You can come in, set up, and leave without a trace.

KIM: Boom, it's a structure. Boom, it's gone.

BROWNING: They can be magical, from hot air balloons to the dancing columns at car lots. Why?

HANSEN: We don't think critically about what is holding up the walls and ceilings of the spaces we are in. We recognize and trust

"The ability to defy gravity, and even to fly, is certainly tied to childhood imagination, but it also persists as a powerful trope for adults, allowing them to imagine alternate realities." —Andrew Blauvelt, "Inflated Realities," Perspecta 42: The Real

Air Dancer.

their solid elements because we have a frame of reference. Inflatables operate on a different logic.

KIM: They are built with materials that we cannot see or touch. They're nothing. You could swallow the material of the Blur Building in Switzerland—the vapor of Lake Neuchatel. In an inflatable, you're breathing its structural elements.

Greta Hansen, Kyung Jae Kim, and Adam Koogler

KOOGLER: They make space tangible by taking the shape of whatever context they're in. You can tie them down with rope, press on them, slap them, and they bounce back.

"The technique of art is to make objects 'unfamiliar,' to make forms difficult, to increase the difficulty and length of perception because the process of perception is an aesthetic end in itself and must be prolonged. Art is a way of experiencing the artfulness of an object; the object is not important."
—Viktor Shklovsky, Art as Technique

HANSEN: They move in time and react to touch, wind, and the space around them. Inflatables are magical structures that electrify their surroundings.

BROWNING: With Doug Meyer of Rustbelt Rebirth, you built a "bicycle blower." The spinning of a bicycle's back wheel activates an exhaust fan that blows air into the bubble. Raumlabor's Spacebuster is also a mobile inflatable pavilion, but it is blown up from the back of a van.

Raumlabor's Spacebuster on Manhattan's Lower East Side, April 2009.

KOOGLER: Ours is a direct response to Space-buster. We reject the car, which is reliant upon the capitalist structures that Occupy protested against. It's heavy and we're light. There's no need for anything external.

HANSEN: We're purists. Making people sweat.

KIM: Cars cannot be driven into public parks. But bikes can go anywhere. They're always welcome.

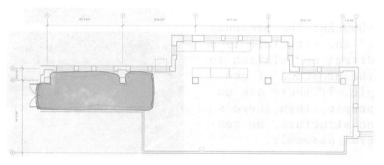

Plan for "bottleneck" Inflatable General Assembly installation at Studio-X New York, October 17, 2013.

BROWNING: You built a 40-foot long "bottleneck" Inflatable General Assembly for the hallway of Studio-X New York. People unzipped and passed through in order to attend an event on the other side. How does Inflatable General Assembly assemble and facilitate direct democracy?

→ fig. 007

HANSEN: You make your own space. If you're here, you're blowing it up. You're part of the constant creation of the space itself. Our ideal model would have multiple bikes with people facing inward, participating in the assembly as they ride and inflate.

KOOGLER: The presence of the structure is a direct correlation to the presence of people. If there are no people, then there's no structure, no general assembly.

BROWNING: On the other side of the bubble, people discussed the occupation of Taksim Gezi Park in Istanbul.

KOOGLER: When testing perfumes, people sniff coffee beans in between. They cleanse

→ figs. 008–010

the nose in the way that ginger cleanses the palate. We thought about people arriving at this event. How do you go from your day job in Manhattan to protesting in Turkey? It seemed bizarre to simply walk into a space and change

the channel. When you unzipped the bubble, you walked into a light space. Some weight may have lifted off your shoulders; maybe you took a deep breath. There's a wiping of the slate, and now you're talking about Turkey. Now you're protesting.

HANSEN: And it's nothing. It's differential air pressure. But inside, you're in another place.

→ figs. 011 & 012

"We walk places that aren't supposed to be walked."

MANDALA: REIMAGINING COLUMBUS CIRCLE
Karen Finley

Karen Finley leads Mandala: Reimagining Columbus Circle.

Historic postcard of Columbus Circle, 1902.

KAREN FINLEY: Mandala, from Sanskrit, meaning circle, is a lens by which to read, understand, and meditate. It can reveal psychic states. The mandala has been used by many cultures. By Tibetans, and by Native Americans, who made sand paintings. Once they were made, they were destroyed. So the mandala is a transitional space, and the process of making one can be transformative.

On Friday, September 26 and Saturday, September 27, 2014, Karen Finley led three groups of twelve people on Mandala: Reimagining Columbus Circle, a participatory walk in and around Manhattan's Columbus Circle, at 12pm, 11am, and 3pm respectively. The walk lasted ninety minutes and required the following materials: camera phones, lollipops, paper, pens, and tape. The text that runs alongside this interview was written by the artist. Unless noted, the following photographs were taken along this walk.

GAVIN BROWNING: What does the mandala mean to you?

FINLEY: Carl Jung would ask his patients a question, then ask them to create. To draw and paint within a circle. He used the mandala as a way for patients to read. The mandalas in his book <u>Mandala</u> are gorgeous. Sometimes they're very abstract geometries. They provide focus, a pictorial language to express chaos, histories, and emotions by assembling visual information and symbols within one circular map.

I also use mandalas as a practice, and I'm interested in reading architecture and urban plans as expressions of psychic states. You can read the symbols in your dreams, but you can also create symbols when you're awake, out of scenes in your life. What can this building, this moment, reveal for my unconscious?

CAITLIN BLANCHFIELD: The mandala is an introspective journey, but the walk you led around Columbus Circle for GSAPP and Elastic City took self-realization to the urban scale.

FINLEY: My exact question was scale. I'm applying psychological, therapeutic, and religious practice to the city as a way of diagnosing. The mandala will reveal, and the person reading through it will speak. The walk revealed complexity.

We meet at the circle and orient ourselves. What is in our mandala? A garden of seasonal plants and trees native to the Carolinas yellow buckeyes, with poisonous fruit. Wooden benches frame and cooperate with comfort. Curved plots of water spray displays that are inspired by the Bellagio fountains, amidst desert speculation sands in Las Vegas. The splashing sound hums out traffic yet offers coolness and displacement from the concrete sky. → fig. 013

Mandala: Reimagining Columbus Circle

My eyes were opened to the history of Columbus Circle, and that gave me joy in being there. Witnessing so many people participating and making the space their own, even amidst the corporations... It felt as if there had been a family secret. Or as if someone had not been telling you something. They're holding back. It's horrible, but when they finally tell you what's bothering them, you feel closer. Once that happens in a relationship, it's always going to be better.

What's exciting is that one can change the mandala. It becomes activist when we reimagine it. When we walk places that aren't supposed to be walked, write and read poems about our personal discoveries, recreate the monuments around us, bring nature into the subway. I thought for sure that walking the

We walk the perimeter of the circle on higher ground and find a pathway through the seasonal plants and sanctuary of poisonous trees. We walk in single file with traffic that moves counterclockwise, as if going back in time. → fig. 014

landscaped perimeter of the circle would be taboo, that we would break the boundaries of access. But surely, the path was there. We did not get stopped. Not even when bringing art down into the subway or taping our monuments to the Columbus monument—and we weren't three people, we were a group. It gave me great joy that there are still spaces to be able to do that.

BROWNING: The circle buzzes with energy. People skateboard, dance, and eat there during the day, and sleep on the steps of the monument and on the encircling benches at night.

BLANCHFIELD: It is next to Central Park, yet people hang out there, in the middle of traffic.

FINLEY: It is wonderful to be in the middle of the hustle and bustle. You're attuned to your surroundings, but there is also a pregnancy within the enclosure. It's as if you're in the womb with activity all around you, and the overpowering noise of water from the fountains. It is known that babies sleep more when the mother is walking around and doing things. I wonder if calm occurs within the circle as well. On that island.

How do we navigate these violent memories cast in marble? → figs. 015 & 016

The homeless sleep and dream on these steps uninterrupted.

BROWNING: Circles appeared many times on our walk.

FINLEY: Usually within architecture, windows are square or rectangular. In urban planning, this is echoed in the grid. Everything is done on the square. But the circle is less used. It's marginalized.

At the Paris Peace Accords in 1973, there was discussion of the shape of the table. The first table was long, and it wasn't working. They had to get a circular table, because change occurs around a circle. There's no beginning or end, and there are no sides. Even those words—"no beginning or end; no sides"—release anxiety. Right there, within that space.

There were many circles on our walk. The pattern of traffic, the placement of buildings, the sun shining through the canopy of trees in Central Park, which had also been planted in a circular grove. I thought it was delightful for us to notice that, because we aren't always so aware. But there is tension between this beauty and America's ugly history. You don't have the whole story at Columbus Circle, and that is what needs to be revealed.

BLANCHFIELD: At 13 feet, the monument to Christopher Columbus is not grand. But it is permanently fixed in the urban fabric. In contrast, the exquisite corpse monuments that we drew in groups were small and ephemeral.

This cosmopolitan center is built on genocide, colonialism, and occupation. It intersects Broadway, which runs past corporation headquarters, universities, the bright lights of theater, where the ball drops and the New Year begins, past Union Square, down to Wall Street and Ground Zero. This broad street was once the Wickquasgeck Trail, a path walked and surveyed by the Lenape.

FINLEY: I'm interested in including time and vulnerability within monuments. Allowing for

time rather than fighting it. I love that the pyramids and Stonehenge are human attempts at understanding mortality. There's beauty and humanity in that. But the designs of many monuments don't equate to human scales of vulnerability. Being a woman, too, I see forms of dominance that equate more with a male body. They always communicate strength. Maya Lin's Vietnam Veterans Memorial is very moving, because it is just the names. But that too is about the strength of the granite coming through the ground.

Blanchfield: The Time Warner Center at 10 Columbus Circle signaled a shift from public space for exchange and debate to the privatization of discourse. Does the walk reassert public conversation?

→ fig. 017

Exquisite corpse monuments drawn by participants.

FINLEY: I think activism occurs by osmosis, just by walking and being there. On the day of the walk, a social media star announced he'd be at Columbus Circle at a certain time, and tons of young kids showed up to take selfies with him by the monument. Were they thinking about activism? No. But they made the space their own.

We study the monument to Columbus. We work in small groups creating our own monument as a replacement. We create exquisite corpses, a Victorian parlor game in which each participant draws a different section. The first draws the head and folds the paper to hide the image, the second draws the body, and the third draws the legs and feet. Mermaids and symbols of social justice. We create collaborative poems to replace sanctioned verse. We hang our designs next to the monument and read our lyrics to the public.

I'm reminded of what was there—an urban renewal project called the Coliseum, a convention center. It was a very grandiose name, considering the

We cross south to CNN and the Museum of Arts and Design, knowing that underneath its façade is the whimsy of the Lollipop Building. We suck on a lolly, looking above and ahead to a liquor store, kiosks, horses and buggies, remnants of phone booths. Dino's Shoe Repair somehow survives.

history of the Coliseum in the ancient world for public viewing. Now it's been replaced by Time Warner and CNN, new coliseums for spectatorship and broadcasting, but private ones. So I think about the development of the circle in terms of readership and audience.

→ fig. 018

But I'm at odds with my own role as a consumer of the media. I was delighted that I crossed Broadway with Don Lemon, for example. I am both a consumer and participant in this portal, this eye of the world. The creep factor of it is surveillance and the corporatization of information. That the world is watching.

The Coliseum and office tower at Columbus Circle, 1956–2000.

BLANCHFIELD: Columbus Circle is also a space of resistance. In the months before and after the walk, protests occurred there around around climate change, police brutality, and the occupation of the West Bank.

FINLEY: Protests and marches don't start at 42nd Street. They don't start at Battery Park City. They start at Columbus Circle. I look at it as a foyer for our city, an entryway for people to meet and begin.

We enter a canopy of trees in Central Park for a respite. We make ninety-second videos of the trees and the sky on our phones, and we gather twigs and leaves. → figs. 019 & 020

BROWNING: Why reimagine this place?

FINLEY: Is it an opportunity to make amends, and to include more voices in Colum-

Everything is measured from here. All mileage from New York City begins and ends here.

bus Circle. I would change the name and hold rituals and ceremonies to activate it in a new way. A festival to bring awareness to what our buildings and landscapes hold, to the sacred trail that was exploited to build Broadway.

BLANCHFIELD: Could you have done this alone?

FINLEY: It has to be activated with others. I meditated by visiting, looking, and seeing the circle by myself beforehand. But it was in the practice of walking as a group, a community, that the benefit occurred. We looked at the individual components of Columbus Circle like items in the refrigerator. How are they going to make a meal? What are the recipes? More people have more knowledge, and the walk was built by many different people.

We pass a monument to the USS Maine, food carts, and hawkers, and cross to a statue of the globe at the northern tip of Columbus Circle. A smaller version of the Unisphere built for the 1964 World's Fair in Flushing Meadows Park in Queens. We make our way to Jazz at Lincoln Center, acknowledging America's greatest art form.

We enter the subway station by escalator. Once below, we find a circle of inlaid tile with the four directional points. We stand together in circle and place our phones on the floor. We intersperse flora with the phones and press play in unison. We hold hands in silence, watching our dream catcher. → figs. 021 & 022

"These works compel us to reconsider how we read and inhabit urban space."

MINGLING IN CURIOUS AND UNCANNY MANNERS
Mabel O. Wilson

Historic postcard of the World Trade Center.

> A tactic is determined by the absence of power just as a strategy is organized by the postulation of power.
> —Michel de Certeau, *The Practice of Everyday Life*

"The ordinary practitioners of the city live 'down below,'" observed Michel de Certeau of the urban denizens of late 1970s Manhattan—the walkers. They moved invisibly through the city, writing and rewriting its text "without being able to read it."[1] Hidden by a labyrinth of streets and passages, the walkers' surreptitious movements "select fragments taken from vast ensembles of production in order to compose new stories with them."[2] Darting about, they craft makeshift stories between cellars, lampposts, steps, window ledges, benches, stoops, curbs, and other pockets of space, stitching together an urban tapestry that pulses with life. Their daily movements, habits, and memories appropriate and short-circuit the logics of the vast urban system—the economic, social, and cultural institutions and structures housed by architecture. Theirs is a tactical appropriation of the city, the urban production built and controlled by capital.

In the steel and glass monuments of power high above those who walk the streets, the "optical artifact" of Manhattan's relentless grid reveals the meaning of the city's text to those "lifted out of the city's grasp."[3] Through the concrete and glass apertures of One World Trade Center—what de Certeau described as "the tallest letter in the world," a depth of field emerges from downtown across the Village and up to midtown Manhattan, bleeding into Central Park.[4] To those ensconced in the towers, the city dematerializes into a pattern of blocks—abstract space represented in aerial photographs, maps, deeds, and ledgers so that it can be measured and studied by the "space planner, urbanist, city planner, or cartographer."[5]

For de Certeau, the abstracted panorama afforded only from the roosts of glass-skinned skyscrapers had become a copy of a city already known through images. Architects, planners, and developers had built a city previously imagined only in drawings, paintings, and film. The World Trade Center towers—designed by Minoru Yamasaki, financed by the Port Authority of New

York and New Jersey, and lobbied for by finance magnate David Rockefeller—represented "a monumental figure of Western urban development."[6] They were a bellwether of other skyscraping letters, prisms, pine cones, torqued cylinders, and a host of algorithmically deformed volumes that would eventually mimic Manhattan's towering ambitions in skylines of cities across the global north and south. If New York City in the 1970s was the urtext of the postmodern city, did the twenty-first-century city fulfill the philosopher's speculation that it would become a referential image of itself—Gotham, the Big Apple, or the Empire City?

The projects in *Group Efforts: Changing Public Space* are participatory and pedagogical endeavors. In different and complementary ways, they reenvision the simulacrum city by appropriating, reframing, and renaming its language. Each propose a new mode of occupying the city, transforming spatial practices and critically engaging how we make and use squares, streets, sidewalks, and buildings. Mandala: Reimagining Columbus Circle by Karen Finley, Subjective Contours by Hayal Pozanti and Todd Shalom, and Inflatable General Assembly by the collective Common Practice prompt us to consider what we might learn by walking the city, and in so doing, crafting new social spaces out of the activities of urban life today. With inequality on the rise, and rights compromised by aggressive policing, these works compel us to reconsider how we read and inhabit urban space. Can we imagine it beyond the meanings imposed by development, leisure, tourism, and mass media?

MEDIATED CITY

Survey New York City's ever-changing architectural stock. Times Square has been revamped into a nostalgic crossroads that never was, a nexus of theme stores and overpriced chain restaurants that cater to the plastic cash of tourists. In Midtown, a new crop of needle-thin residential high-rises offers wealthy non-residents a slice of the skyline with sweeping views of Central Park below. Neighborhoods in all five boroughs have been overtaken by resettlers hoping to recreate the hip hominess of their favorite sitcoms, from rerun standbys like *Sex in the City* to a new generation of *Girls*.

Gone is the city government that sanctioned Robert Moses's grand plans of urban renewal. The powerbroker and his minions built a modern metropolis of residential towers, civic plazas, public convention centers, parkways, parks, beaches, and bridges. It was a mid-century machine that was meant to manufacture and liberate ideal citizenry from grime and discordant ethnic, racial, and class factionalism. But, not all neighborhoods received equal shares of governmental benevolence, such as the Lower East Side, the tenements of which were settled by waves of migrants and immigrants arriving to find work in the manufacturing sector. As New York deindustrialized, moving its industry first to the suburban fringe, then out of state, and eventually overseas, the city became home to finance, insurance, real estate, and media corporations that possessed a different set of ambitions than did those of urban reformers.[7]

These service sector industries crafted a new image of the city—one envisioned by architects at the behest of real estate developers, the private overlords of the late-capitalist city. Public-private partnerships, the neoliberal privatization of the city's building initiatives, have mostly benefitted the bottom line of the latter. With their rise, state-sponsored efforts to build high-rises for the poor and middle class were replaced by sleek glass towers for newly minted Wall Street millionaires. Public parks have been traded for Privately Owned Public Spaces (POPS), and roadways, subways, and other shared amenities (such as a robust and egalitarian school system) have deteriorated as city tax coffers shrink and the elite offshore their wealth to lighten their personal and corporate tax burdens. The airbrushed allure of twenty-first-century New York City on billboards and websites hawking luxury lifestyles—"the intersection of what you do and where you want to be," claims a promotional website for the Hudson Yards megaproject on Manhattan's West Side—is a thin veil for the economic, social, and political inequalities endured by a large number of less fortunate but nonetheless hard-working residents.

OPTICAL CITY

Columbus Circle lies at the western and southern edges of Central Park, where Broadway meets 59th Street and 8th Avenue. For over a century, it has been an arena to express individual and collective aspirations and where local, national, and now global ideals are proffered to the public. The circle has undergone many transformations, including the construction of the massive New York Coliseum in the mid-1950s. A Moses-era urban renewal initiative financed by the Metropolitan Transportation Authority (MTA), the edifice functioned as an exhibition hall for American-made goods, until those goods were no longer manufactured in this country.[8] In the late 1990s, the MTA sold the land beneath the Coliseum for $350 million to the real estate development company Related Companies and the media conglomerate AOL-Time Warner. Ten years later the hall was demolished and replaced by a $1.7 billion retail, hotel, dining, office, and media hub: the Time Warner Center. Designed by David Childs of Skidmore, Owings and Merrill (SOM), it was opened to the public in 2003.[9] Many of the television shows that are filmed within this building regularly broadcast views of the manicured circle outside. The center's two residential towers, the reflective blue glass of which disappears against the sky, have become vertical space-deposit boxes for wealthy foreign investors. Several of the towers' peripatetic residents have siphoned monies out of their shaky national economies to park cash in apartments with panoramic views of the city, albeit ones they rarely enjoy.[10] Today, these voyeurs join Christopher Columbus in gazing down upon his namesake circle.

Mandala, the walk that Karen Finley led in October 2014, intervened upon the representations of power, conquest, domination, and desire that are embedded within this bustling node. Her walks, sponsored by GSAPP and Elastic City, reread and reimagined the site by leading groups of twelve participants on a participatory excursion around Columbus Circle and its neighboring environs. (I joined one of the walks.) Like de Certeau, Finley taps into the unconscious movements of pedestrians—the locals, tourists, and workers who move in and about Columbus Circle unaware of the manifestations of power strategically symbolized and operative in its terrain—by forming a mandala. According to the artist, this reinscribes individual associations within the circular urban form.

We began by walking an outer ledge between the plantings of a landscape created by the firm Olin Partnership. Landscapers typically traverse this hidden path, and walking it provided us with a view of the site that is rarely experienced by pedestrians. We gathered around the central monument to share observations of the medallions and bas-relief plaques affixed to the column that supports the Columbus statue.[11] Inch by inch, we decoded the language of conquest that the monument projects into the plaza. Split into groups of three, we put pen to paper to craft exquisite corpse drawings derived from interpretations and unconscious associations. In the same surrealist style, we wrote poems. When read aloud, the words created a new assemblage, a poetic recalibration of site. A parlor game became tactical ruse in what de Certeau describes as "putting one over on the adversary on his won turf, hunter's tricks, maneuverable, poly-morph mobilities, jubilant, poetic, and warlike discoveries."[12]

This corner of the city is also where architecture meets infrastructure and natural cycles—the busy multilevel subway transfer point below ground, the flora and fauna of Central Park above ground. There, we used cellphones to capture ninety-second videos of the brilliantly colored fall tree canopy. Later, we placed our phones on the tiled floor of the subway station below and played these twelve videos back. It was a multi-screen, temporal performance of the changing landscape above. Our videos produced a multi-perspective view of Central Park's periphery. Each tiny screen pixelated the monocular view of the park produced by the security and television cameras that scan the plaza on a round-the-clock basis.

Mandala cast the edges, corners, sections, and symbolic meanings of Columbus Circle into new light and configuration. This new spatial rendering of the circle, a mandala created by our movements, allowed me to imagine other ways to read a dynamic city. "The great plate-glass front had turned to a deep blue, the color of a Maxfield Parrish moonlight—a blue that seemed to press close upon the pane as if to crowd its way into the restaurant," wrote F. Scott Fitzgerald. "Dawn had come up in Columbus Circle, magical, breathless dawn, silhouetting the great statue of the immortal Christopher, and mingling in a curious and uncanny manner with the fading yellow electric light inside."[13]

HAPTIC CITY

Hayal Pozanti and Todd Shalom also plumb the conscious and unconscious dimensions of walking the city. The walk that they led, Subjective Contours, focused less on visible and symbolic dimensions, and more on the haptic experience of the city, this time, the West Village. In *The Death and Life of Great American Cities*, Jane Jacobs hailed the Village for its community, parks, street life, and self-governance, while launching a scathing critique of urban renewal to halt the wrecking balls and bulldozers that were poised to cut a swath through it for a metropolitan artery.[14] As artists moved south to Soho in the 1960s and east to the East Village in the 1980s, the quaint, iconoclastic, and bohemian enclave became a major tourist destination. It was ripe for gentrification. Today, the median price of a residence in the neighborhood hovers around $2.9 million, yet the myth of the Village as a haven for creative strivers persists in the popular imagination.[15] In order to feed public obsession with television shows and movies, companies such as On Location Tours employ actors as guides, offering sightseers authentic experiences of pretend places like Central Perk and Carrie Bradshaw's brownstone.[16]

Subjective Contours took participants up Waverly Street from 6th Avenue and into a loop that included 12th, 13th, and Jane Streets. Pozanti and Shalom asked participants to flatten their view of the city by tracing outlines of buildings onto a clear sheet of acetate. The transparency afforded makers a glimpse of light, texture, and color from the buildings beyond. The accrual of lines and angles that layer one building atop another defamiliarized iconic neighborhood views. The act of drawing flattened the perspectival view of the city, crafting new and imaginary contours from its landscapes. In many ways, this method is the opposite of architectural drawing, which projects the real from an orthographic plane of abstraction. A similar exercise required individuals to trace words discovered in situ onto acetate, an exquisite corpse of poetic verse about the neighborhood.

Walkers explored the tactility of the streetscape by using their bodies as tools of measurement, and their gestures were memorialized with lines of tape. Elsewhere, Pozanti and Shalom asked participants to probe and caress a façade, thereby reconnecting to the human labor that built it. On 7th Avenue, the group sang a score based on the rhythm of windows that lined a block. Deeper in the Village, they crafted a new construction out of string to connect two pieces of street furniture and deposited wishes for the neighborhood into a mailbox. Each movement carved away a new moment and space from the cityscape. Instead of remaining in the unconscious realm of habit, Subjective Contours drew these new spaces into an abstract plane for reflection. The outcome? A poetic interpretation of the West Village that generates new meaning from its urban geometries and architectural materiality, not well-worn media imagery.

PUBLIC CITY

The stock of public space in New York City has been reduced in part due to its privatization by property developers and corporate owners. This contraction of publically owned open space has perhaps been the most transformed through the creation of several hundred POPS by developers in exchange for revised setback and height restrictions and other zoning regulations. Rather than reimagine existing conditions, Common Practice's Inflatable General Assembly (IGA) proposes a new space, a

moveable diaphanous commons for meaningful political delib-
eration and social engagement. Emerging from the fall 2011
occupation of a privately-owned plaza—Zuccotti Park, located
across from the behemoth World Trade Center development
in Lower Manhattan—the pavilion's various prototypes annex
open areas in New York City to redress the diminishing access
to places for political action across the city.

In the 1960s, the New York City government began to offer
incentives for property developers constructing new buildings.
These benefits were offered in exchange for the creation of
spaces—plazas, atria, arcades, gallerias, widened sidewalks and
other spaces—that would be accessible to the general public.[17]
POPS are "an amenity provided and maintained by a developer
for public use, in exchange for additional floor area" that achieve
the criteria "easily seen and read as open to the public" through
the presence of space-defining planter boxes, wide pathways,
and other design features.[18] The appearance of accessibility,
a visual register, supersedes the rights granted to the public
in government-owned public spaces. POPS offer seating for
small groups and individuals—the antithesis to wide-open public spaces such as Union Square and Central Park, which large
crowds can appropriate for rallies and protests (even though
these two iconic places are also now maintained by private Business Improvement Districts [BIDs] and conservancies). With
their requisite furniture, planters, and water features, POPS
are primarily devoted to the pursuit of leisure activities, such
as sipping a latte or finding shade under the trees.

An early POPS, Zuccotti Park was built as Liberty Plaza
Park in front of the headquarters of United States Steel Company's 1 Liberty Plaza (1968), designed by SOM. The park's
latest owner is Brookfield Properties, a real estate development company. The destruction of de Certeau's letters in 2001
greatly damaged the park, and it reopened with a new design
by Cooper, Robertson and Partners in 2006.[19] The refurbished
park added long granite benches that joined the existing high-
cultural marker, artist Mark di Suvero's red bundle of steel,
Joie de Vivre (1997), as well as *Double Check* (1982), a banal

bronze businessman with briefcase by John Seward Johnson II that neither challenges nor offends passersby.

By reclaiming privatized public space for politics, Occupy Wall Street sparked a worldwide protest against growing economic and social inequalities—conditions wrought by reckless corporate greed and abetted by governmental failure to regulate or punish wrongdoing. Used mostly by local workers as an open-air lunchroom or a site for tourists to take respite before embarking to the World Trade Center memorial site, protestors transformed the 33,000 square foot park into a hive of political and social activity. Common Practice's initial proposal to inflate a tent over a block-length section of the public rally makes its improvisational spirit tangible and architectural. While buildings tend to be long term and permanent, the soft architecture of the IGA is short term and temporary, a twenty-first-century nomadic armature for the commons.

Common Practice developed and tested several IGA prototypes around New York City, including Pier 4 of the Brooklyn Army Terminal, the entry hall of GSAPP's Studio-X New York in Soho, and Seward Park and Sara D. Roosevelt Park on the Lower East Side. Countercultural movements of the 1960s and 1970s also adopted inflatable architecture. Of note, Archigram undertook similar experiments with inflatables although these were never built. The architects scaled their technologically mutable armatures Suitaloon (1964) and Cushicle (1967) to the body. These projects and others were retreats, inflatable hermitages from onslaught of smog and constant threats of social upheaval. IGA takes a slightly different direction. To inflate the IGA depends upon a fan charged by the physical energy of a person pedaling a bicycle. In this way, the collective space of public action, the polis, must be made and remade by its individuals.

POLITICAL CITY

"The street," writes Rebecca Solnit, "is democracy's greatest arena, the place where ordinary people can speak, unsegregated by walls, unmediated by those with more power."[20] New York City's streets and public spaces continue to register political participation. Two months after I walked with others around Columbus Circle, fellow New Yorkers protested the failure of the judicial system to indict the killers of Eric Garner, an unarmed African-American man choked to death by New York City police officers arresting him for selling loose cigarettes on a Staten Island sidewalk. The Black Lives Matter movement has emerged in response to this and other callous acts of violence against unarmed African-American men and women. Adopting the tactics of other Black Lives Matter protests staged around the world, groups around the city have lain prostrate in Grand Central Terminal and City Hall and marched on the Brooklyn Bridge, Times Square, and other major streets and public squares. Die-ins, a global gesture emblematic of the State's failure to guarantee the basic protections to ensure life, have turned the simulacrum city into sites of political action.

At the December 13, 2014 Millions March NYC protest, a large banner of Garner's eyes, created by the artist JR, led phalanxes of protestors. Circulating widely on social media and mainstream media channels, the oversized image of the victim's eyes carried palpable and powerful weight that challenged the stereotype of the dangerous and foreboding black brute. The techniques of image production in the mediated city can become tactical tools mobilized by walkers to challenge those in power. By overtaking the connective tissue of the city—from highways encamped with protestors to train stations floored with die-ins—bodies usurped the power of privatized public space and commanded the omniscient lens of media empires. In the process, such actions showed the resilient and resistant capacity of social life to the oppressive forces of capital-driven development.

A die-in at Grand Central Terminal, 2014.

In a similar spirit, the projects in this book reinvigorate the street and the square as vital political and social spheres. The creators and the participants generated a critical space for collaborative engagement to reimagine and remake what the city could be, who might live here, and its significance. Somewhere between the individual and the collective, the scale of the groups that they gather implies intimacy and performs the labor of meaning-making. Done together at a specific time, they generate space for collaboration. The politics so pregnant within are of a different, though sympathetic, strain to those expressions of solidarity and dissent. Their aim is not to make the city seen to itself, but rather through tactical appropriation to make it heard, touched, and felt.

1   Michel De Certeau, *The Practice of Everyday Life* (Berkeley, CA: University of California Press, 1984), 35.

2   De Certeau, *The Practice of Everyday Life*, 35.

3   De Certeau, *The Practice of Everyday Life*, 92.

4   De Certeau, *The Practice of Everyday Life*, 93.

5   De Certeau, *The Practice of Everyday Life*, 93.

6   De Certeau, *The Practice of Everyday Life*, 93.

7   Robert Fitch, *The Assassination of New York* (New York: Verso, 1996).

8   Christopher Gray, "Streetscapes: The Coliseum; The 'Hybrid Pseudo Modern' on Columbus Circle," *New York Times*, April 26, 1987.

9   Charles V. Bagli, "A Deal Is Struck For Coliseum Site," *New York Times*, July 28, 1998.

10   Louise Story and Stephanie Saul, "Towers of Secrecy: Stream of Foreign Wealth Flows to Elite New York Real Estate," *New York Times*, February 7, 2015.

11   The monument of Christopher Columbus sits 75 feet above the busy intersection. The marble statue, carved by Gaetano Russo and erected in 1892 to mark the 400 year anniversary of Columbus's landing in the Americas, allowed New York City's growing Italian community to celebrate its European heritage and the contribution of Italians to the founding of the nation. The monument enshrines the 13-foot-tall Columbus as an explorer who inaugurated the colonial expansion of Europe into new regions of the globe.

12   De Certeau, *The Practice of Everyday Life*, 40.

13   F. Scott Fitzgerald, *May Day, Babylon Revisited and Other Stories* (New York: Scribner Classic/Collier, 1987), 67.

14   Jane Jacobs, *The Death and Life of Great American Cities* (New York: Random House, 1961), 127.

15   On March 2, 2015, the median sales price of a home in Greenwich Village was $2,822,500 according to the website Trulia.

16   De Certeau's claim that the city would become a copy of its own image can be confirmed by the activities of actress Sarah Jessica Parker, who like her television character Carrie Bradshaw, laid claim to a stoop in the Village. In 2015, she sold the property for $20 million.

17   Department of City Planning, City of New York, "A Primer
for Public Plazas," www.nyc.gov/
html/dcp/html/pops/pops_history.
shtml.

18   Department of City Planning, City of New York, "Publicly
Owned Private Spaces," www.
nyc.gov/html/dcp/html/pops/pops.
shtml.

19   Douglas Kellner, "9/11,
Spectacles of Terror, and Media
Manipulation: A Critique of
Jihadist and Bush Media Politics,"
Critical Discourse Studies, vol. 1,
no. 1 (2004), 41–64.

20   Rebecca Solnit, *Wanderlust:
A History of Walking* (New York:
Penguin, 2001), 216.

Image Credits

Hayal Pozanti and
Todd Shalom, Subjective
Contours

Pp. 12-13 courtesy of
Hayal Pozanti

Figs. 001-006 and p. 22
courtesy of Justin Liu,
Columbia University GSAPP

P. 20 courtesy of Emily
Oppenheim

Greta Hansen, Kyung
Jae Kim, and Adam Koogler,
Inflatable General
Assembly

Pp. 29, 30, and 37
courtesy of Common
Practice

P. 32 courtesy of Artúr
van Balen

P. 34 courtesy of Chip
Lord

Figs. 007-012 and p. 26
© Justin Beck

P. 36 courtesy of Alan
Tansey

Karen Finley, Mandala:
Reimagining Columbus
Circle

Pp. 43 and 50 courtesy of
Seymour B. Durst Old York
Library Collection. Avery
Architectural & Fine
Arts Library, Columbia
University

Figs. 013-022 and p. 42
courtesy of Justin Liu,
Columbia University GSAPP

Mabel O. Wilson, *Mingling in
Curious and Uncanny Manners*

P. 72 courtesy of Seymour
B. Durst Old York Library
Collection. Avery Architectural
& Fine Arts Library, Columbia
University

P. 83 courtesy of Khurran Paravaz

Biographies

HAYAL POZANTI was born in Istanbul in 1983 and lives and works in New York City. She has been featured in Prospect 3, the New Orleans biennial, and is in the collections of JP Morgan, the Los Angeles County Museum of Art (LACMA) and the Eli and Edythe Broad Art Museum. Pozanti is known for her acrylic paintings, animated GIFs, and sculptures—all of which are based on an invented alphabet that generates anthropomorphic forms.

TODD SHALOM works with text, sound, and image to re-contextualize the body in space using vocabulary of the everyday. He is the founder and director of Elastic City. In this role, Todd leads his own walks, collaborates with artists to lead joint walks, and works with artists in a variety of disciplines to adapt their expertise to the participatory walk format. His work has been presented by the Abrons Art Center, Brooklyn Museum, The Invisible Dog, ISSUE Project Room, Museum of Modern Art, New Museum, P.S. 122, and Printed Matter. He is a member of the core faculty in Pratt Institute's MFA in Writing.

GRETA HANSEN is co-founder of Common Practice and Warm Engine, experimental design practices that have focused on subjects ranging from food to protest strategies to national building typology. She has taught design studios at the New Jersey Institute of Technology and Universidade de São José in Macau. She is affiliated with the Lab at Rockwell Group and the design-build company Wolfgang and Hite.

KYUNG JAE KIM, AIA, is an urban designer, architect, artist, and co-founder of Common Practice. He has a wide range of interests converging at the meeting point of art, architecture, and planning, as well as new uses of architectural drawing in the digital age. In 2014, he co-founded Architecture Work Office. He practices architecture in New York.

ADAM KOOGLER is an architect and educator living in Brooklyn, New York and co-founder of Common Practice along with Greta Hansen and Kyung Jae Kim. He works with SHoP Architects, contributes to CLOG magazine, and has taught design studios at the University of Cincinnati, New York Institute of Technology, and Pratt Institute.

Born in Chicago, KAREN FINLEY received her MFA from the San Francisco Art Institute. She is the author of eight books, including The Reality Shows and a 25th anniversary edition of Shock Treatment. Her recent work includes Artists Anonymous, a social practice self-help open meeting for those addicted to art, presented at Museum of Arts and Design; Written in Sand, a performance of music and her writings on AIDS; Open Heart, a Holocaust memorial at Camp Gusen, Austria; Broken Negative, where Finley reconsiders her infamous chocolate performance that brought her to the Supreme Court; and at the New Museum, Sext Me if You Can. A recipient of many awards and grants, including a Guggenheim Fellowship, Finley is an arts professor in Art and Public Policy at New York University.

As the Nancy and George E. Rupp Professor, MABEL O. WILSON teaches architectural design and history/ theory courses at Columbia University GSAPP. She is also appointed as a Research Fellow at the Institute for Research in African American Studies and co-directs Global Africa Lab. She is the author of Negro Building: Black Americans in the World of Fairs and Museums,

a runner-up for the John Hope Franklin Prize for best American Studies publication in 2012. Her scholarly essays have appeared in numerous journals and books on critical geography, memory studies, art and architecture. She is a founding member of Who Builds Your Architecture?, an advocacy project to educate the architectural profession about the problems of globalization and labor.

GAVIN BROWNING is Director of Events and Public Programs at Columbia University GSAPP. Previously, he directed Studio-X New York, where he organized events and exhibitions, and edited The Studio-X New York Guide. He wrote and co-produced the animated short The Commons, and his independent work has been supported by the Graham Foundation for Advanced Studies in the Fine Arts. He holds a BA in English from The New School and a MS in Urban Planning from Columbia University.

Acknowledgements

Thank you to Dean Amale
Andraos for her guid-
ance and support. Also at
GSAPP, David Hinkle, my
co-producer Paul Dallas,
and James Graham and
Caitlin Blanchfield in the
Office of Publications,
whose careful readings
helped to shape this book.
Neil Donnelly's graphic
design is beautiful. Thank
you to Mabel O. Wilson for
her thoughtful contribu-
tion; Justin Beck, Justin
Liu, and Emily Oppenheim
for their images; the people who participated in
these projects; and George
and Margie Browning for
their participation from
afar. It has been an
honor to work with Karen
Finley, Greta Hansen,
Kyung Jae Kim, Adam
Koogler, Hayal Pozanti,
and Todd Shalom. I dedi-
cate this book to Rachel
Guidera (1972-2014).
—G.B.

SERIES EDITORS
James Graham &
Caitlin Blanchfield

VOLUME EDITOR
Gavin Browning

SERIES DESIGN
Neil Donnelly &
Stefan Thorsteinsson

VOLUME DESIGN
Neil Donnelly &
Sean Yendrys

COPY EDITOR
Walter Ancarrow

PRINTER
Die Keure

GSAPP BOOKS
An imprint of The Graduate
School of Architecture,
Planning and Preservation
Columbia University
1172 Amsterdam Ave.
407 Avery Hall
New York, NY 10027

Visit our website at
arch.columbia.edu/books

GSAPP Books distributed by
Columbia University Press
at cup.columbia.edu

This book has been pro-
duced through the Office
of the Dean, Amale
Andraos, and the Office
of Print Publications.

ISBN 978-1-941332-10-8

LIBRARY OF CONGRESS CATALOGING-
IN-PUBLICATION DATA
Group efforts : changing
public space / edited by Gavin
Browning ; with an essay by
Mabel O. Wilson.
    pages cm. —
(GSAPP Transcripts)
    Subjective Contours / Hayal
Pozanti and Todd Shalom --
Inflatable General Assembly /
Greta Hansen, Kyung Jae Kim,
and Adam Koogler -- Mandala:
Reimagining Columbus Circle /
Karen Finley -- Mingling in
Curious and Uncanny Manners /
Mabel O. Wilson.
    ISBN 978-1-941332-10-8
1. Public spaces--
Social aspects. 2. Space
(Architecture)--Social
aspects. I. Browning, Gavin,
editor. II. Wilson, Mabel
(Mabel O.) Mingling in curious
and uncanny manners.
    NA9053.S6.G76 2015
    701'.8--dc23

2015021556